Pam Chapuisat

KT-492-431

Sportsviewers Guide
DARTS

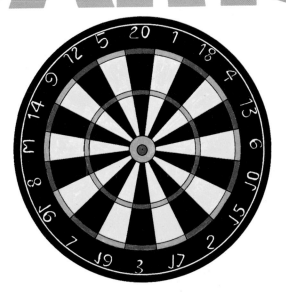

Peter Bills

DAVID & CHARLES
Newton Abbot   London

Contents

**British Library Cataloguing in
Publication Data**
Bills, Peter
    Darts. — (Sportsviewers guides)
    1. Darts (Game) — History
    I. Title   II. Series
    794.3′09   GV1565

ISBN 0–7153–8502–X

The Sportsviewers' Guide to Darts
was produced and designed by
Siron Publishing Limited of
20 Queen Anne Street, London W1,
Series editor: Nicholas Keith
Photographs by Tommy Hindley and
Tony Henshaw of Professional Sport.

Typeset by ABM Typographics Ltd, Hull
and printed by
Printer Industria Gráfica SA
Cuatro Caminos, Apartado 8,
Sant Vicenç dels Horts,
Barcelona, Spain DLB 17343-1983
for David & Charles (Publishers) Limited
Brunel House   Newton Abbot   Devon

Foreword

From the *Mayflower* to Wembley Conference Centre.

From double top to Annie's room.

From teenagers' championship to world professional.

From London to Singapore.

From me to you.

Certainly the contents of this book give the necessary basics for the beginner — from rules to techniques and to the course any future champion must take if he or she wishes to reach the top bracket. For the connoisseur, it provides a who's who of the darts world with their views and comments.

The vision of Olly Croft, the British Darts Organisation's general secretary, is now reality and has given the chance for all dart players to show their skills. The vision was continued by the editor of sport at BBC Manchester, Nick Hunter, who has shown great faith and expertise in darts. He introduced the split screen and has given many memorable moments of the skills, anguish and triumphs of those players to the armchair viewers, now in their millions, in this fast and exciting sport.

Darts is the fastest growing spectator sport and also has the most participants (around 7 million players) in Great Britain today. Read on and see where it all began and what it has achieved right to the present day.

Tony Green

History and development

The story of darts has been one of the great sporting successes in the last decade – largely thanks to television. It has grown from a working class pastime in British pubs to an international sport with a TV audience of millions. The cry 'one hundred and eighty' has become a catch phrase.

Those who created the initial movements in the game which was to become known as darts could be forgiven a disbelieving blink at its progress in the latter half of the twentieth century. Not only the instigators of the sport would be surprised; workers who threw darts at pub walls to alleviate dark moments in the first threequarters of this century would express amazement, almost total disbelief, at the rapid expansion of the game.

Darts has become big business, giving the lie to those who thought it would remain forever a simple game for the predominately working classes in the public houses of Britain – originally a pastime for warriors in their free time, relaxing from battle.

Tracing the development of darts is relatively easy. As recently as the end of the 1960s, the game was virtually unknown in a professional sense, and it offered small earnings to players hoping to make a career from it. In the early 1970s, darts boomed in an extraordinary and unexpected manner. Projection on television brought a vast audience and new potential participants.

Previously players were largely unknown outside the darts world. Television changed all that, providing a base of interest which in turn attracted sponsors. Exhibitions were played in the clubs long before TV became involved. But without the publicity, fees were minimal by comparison with those charged once the leading competitors became known. Television provided the game and the leading characters with an opportun-

ity to market themselves nationally and internationally.

The attraction of the professional ranks was the opportunity to earn good money from a pastime previously looked upon as no more than a leisure activity, a hobby. The thought of earning a living from the sport was new. Big cash incentives are now available to all the game's leading contestants. Ironically that financial development may link the game with its earliest times, because there is every likelihood that from the first it involved small wagers among the players.

The game's first mention dates back to the Middle Ages in England. English bowmen were regarded as the finest exponents of their art in the world and there is a logical progression from creating weapons of war – fighting instruments – to small spearlike pieces used for leisure. These smaller 'weapons' may originally have been used in close-quarter skirmishes. Soldiers played the game, it is believed, not only to pass the time during long campaigns, but to keep their eyesight in trim. Throwing darts at a board some distance away—and having a competition for those who could throw most accurately—seems a plausible recreation for the English bowmen of that time.

Crude 'darts' are said to have been used by the Pilgrim Fathers on board the *Mayflower* as they sailed to the New World in 1620, but the roots of modern darts are in the 19th century. Indeed the game marked time in the 17th and 18th centuries, when there was little development and its history is obscure.

The Industrial Revolution and development of the working classes in factories throughout Britain furthered the cause of darts. Many sports gained momentum in 19th century Britain, with formal rules and governing bodies established and in the late

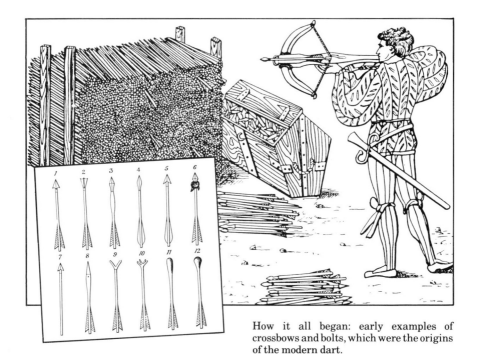

How it all began: early examples of crossbows and bolts, which were the origins of the modern dart.

1800s darts made rapid strides. By the turn of the century, the game was ready to move ahead and develop its present format.

An invention—part-English, part-American—was put forward involving a metal barrel on the stem of the dart (inevitably British and a by-product of the Industrial Revolution) and a paper-flight model from the other side of the Atlantic. The two ideas, married together, laid the foundation of the modern dart. From times when the game was played anywhere, at any time—with crude weapons and the end of a log as a rough sort of board—the game was be coming refined and more technical.

The World Wars of 1914–18 and 1939–45 quickened the pace of the game's development, because of its popularity among servicemen in their off-duty hours. The link between the game and the English public house is another product of the association between darts and the working class. The public houses were frequented mostly by the workers and the game caught on as a lively aspect of pub life. It still retains that association although greater prosperity among the working classes since the end of the Second World War has meant the game has become increasingly popular in people's homes, a comparatively rare aspect in earlier years.

The accepted arrangement of numbers around the board seems to date from 1896 when Brian Gamlin, a Bury carpenter, produced the present system. Of course, the use of numbers on the board—or log-end or simple target of wood from centuries past—was in operation from darts' earliest times.

The year 1908 was important for the game, thanks to the wisdom of magistrates in the Yorkshire industrial centre of Leeds. They presided over a test case to decide whether the game was one of skill or chance. This may seem a light-hearted interlude in the game's history but it was crucial to its rapid growth. The reason was that, if deemed a game of skill, darts could be played on licensed premises. The game owes a great debt to the prowess of a local landlord called Foot Anakin who, it is reported, threw at the board in such splendid style and form that the magistrates were convinced.

The First World War witnessed a rapid expansion; the game went from strength to strength thereafter and by 1924 a committee of licensees was formed into a body named the National Darts Association (NDA). The association declared the game to be: 'The working man's sport; it is cheap, clean and skilful.'

By 1928, such was the growing popularity that a national darts competition was instigated, sponsored by a London Sunday newspaper, the *News of the World*. The name is synonymous with the game of darts and the tournament has continued to this day, interrupted only by the war years of 1939–45. The *News of the World* is still a blue riband event in professional darts.

The boom at the start of the 1970s was signified by the start of another organisation, the British Darts Organisation (BDO). This body has now become more influential than the NDA in the professional sphere although both organisations continue to do sterling work in pursuit and promotion of increased interest in the game of darts.

Long before the BDO came into being, darts had been refined over and over again. Wooden darts disappeared in favour of the metal variety; shafts, now made with aluminium alloy, began to be screwed into the barrel. The technical experts were taking

over.

Since the 1970s the game has burgeoned not only in Britain—where there are now believed to be somewhere around seven million players— but throughout the world. From a game born of the humblest origins, darts became truly international. The appeal of the game is universal: Americans, Swedes, Australians and Belgians are challenging British supremacy in the professional game. Darts is progressing rapidly in countries such as New Zealand and Australia.

Although those countries have no current players to match British masters such as Eric Bristow, Jocky Wilson, John Lowe and Keith Deller, it may be merely a matter of time before they produce players capable of rivalling the best. From Australia to New Zealand, Sweden to Belgium, Abu Dhabi to Bahrein, New York to California, the Phillipines to the Netherlands, players are spreading the game in popularity and appeal.

Tony Brown, one of the UK's leading competitors, believes the time will come when countries hitherto regarded as rank outsiders will produce world champions of their own: 'People who have played in the British Isles have gone out to these other countries and spread the message. Now those countries are gradually finding stars of their own.

'Of course, darts is still in its infancy in many countries but, in years to come, the current feeling that British players have to beat only one or two foreign players to remove the foreign challenge altogether will apply no more. Practically all countries now play some form of darts; there were teams from as far away as Hong Kong in the last world championships. The Phillipines is another country where it is booming. Things are only just getting going over there but they, too,

will become very enthusiastic in time.'

But Brown is convinced the United States will provide the greatest challenge in the years ahead. 'We shall all have to watch out when the Americans catch up at some stage in the future. They have the money and the facilities to promote the game in a really big way. Their only disadvantage is the same suffered by the Australians—distance. It prevents their best players playing regularly against each other which you need to do to improve your standard.

'That is one enormous advantage darts players in the United Kingdom have. In the States, they tend to play in little pockets on whichever coast they live. That is all right for creating interest and spreading the game. But they do not meet often enough to improve themselves against the best players.'

Australia is making conscious efforts to boost the game. The emergence on that vast continent of English-style 'pubs' has undoubtedly helped to 'import' the game into 'Aussie' social life.

In 1982 Bristow and Maureen Flowers, spent a month touring Australia, playing exhibition matches to enthusiastic audiences. In conjunction with the tour, the Australian TV mogul Kerry Packer—better known in the United Kingdom for his World Series Cricket which divided the cricket world in the late 1970s— launched a special eight-week series on darts. More tours are expected for the future and the trail opened by Bristow and Flowers will be followed by other leading stars.

Brisbane is scheduled to stage the 1985 world championships but it had to overcome two determined challengers—Denmark and, surprisingly, Jamaica. Belgium became one of the first countries of Europe to take a professional interest in the game with the creation of the Belgian Darts Federation in 1959. That body is the oldest in Europe outside Britain although few Belgian darts players are yet known internationally.

Stefan Lord led the Swedish darts boom by becoming *News of the World* champion in the UK in both 1978 and 1980, thus winning one of Britain's most prestigious events. In Sweden two major leagues were created for competition following the formation of the Swedish Darts Association in 1973. Now, the number of active players is between five and ten thousand, with interest increasing.

Organisation

The governing body of darts at a professional level in the United Kingdom is the British Darts Organisation (BDO). It was formed by its current secretary, Olly Croft, in January 1973, although the idea was born at a pub in Congleton, Cheshire, at 5am one autumn morning in 1972. The first tournament was the 1973 Home International near Bristol followed by the first World Masters in 1974.

The game developed rapidly between 1976 and 1978, when it won recognition by television. Yorkshire Television showed the indoor league and one of the producers was Sid Waddell. The first network presentation was the Winmau World masters on ITV in 1976. Then BBC screened five days of continual coverage of the first Embassy world professional championship in 1978.

The faith of the television companies has been rewarded by the viewing figures: for the 1983 world final between Deller and Bristow the peak figure was 7·8m—and that at a time when TV audiences were declining sharply for other sports such as soccer.

Croft had played darts for ten years before embarking upon organising the game at professional level. He remembers: 'I first got involved in darts when I went into a pub one Christmas and was bored sitting down talking. I started throwing darts and it all took off from there.'

Croft was born in 1929 and in 1983 he completed his first decade as darts official organiser. He looks after as many as ninety-five events in Britain in a year. He works seven days a week and he is helped by the BDO chairman, Ken Glidle from Coventry and the finance director, Arnold Westlake from Norwich. Croft has a full-time staff of six—two drivers, a secretary's assistant, two typists and the secretary, himself.

Officials like Glidle and Westlake do full-time jobs in other fields but Croft admits: 'They spend so much of their spare time helping run the darts organisation, that in time I feel we shall have to have full-time proper paid officials in those two posts. It is asking a lot of people to give up so much of their free time although, of course, both men like it.'

Croft denies drink is any problem to darts or its image. 'Of course, drink is synonymous with darts, you cannot get away from that aspect. But I don't see it as a problem. The majority of players do not have a problem with drink. Even the few who have have got over the problem. It is not in players' interests to drink too much. Jocky Wilson, for example, has controlled his drinking now.'

Perhaps the major danger to darts and its increasing popularity is overkill on television. Croft and his officials are aware of the risk. 'We know we shall have to control very carefully the amount of darts shown on TV. Games like snooker have been overkilled by too much television coverage. But I don't believe darts has reached that stage yet.

'When clips are shown, they are usually restricted to one or two slots in an entire day. In snooker, sometimes there have been three or four visits in a single evening to a tournament—which we would never allow. It is too much for one sport.'

The BDO has the powers to ban the cameras if it gets to the point where they believe too much is being seen of the game on TV, 'But apart from the world professional championships, you normally only get one slot at a time on TV,' Croft says.

Croft believes darts will continue to flourish but officials must be found to maintain the work done around the country at county level. 'Provided these officials can be found to give their spare time and do useful work, I

Backroom boys and girls at the British Darts Organisation's offices

think darts will go on increasing in popularity. These workers are dedicated and they provide a vital base for the game at a grass roots level.'

The need for professional organisation was quickly apparent to Croft when he become involved in the administrative side of darts. 'It was terribly disorganised at that time; there wasn't even an England team,' he recalls. 'Only four counties had teams and we had to create a world championship to offer incentive for the players to go through to the highest level. At that time, a lot of players did not even cross county borders to play opponents—that was how parochial and underdeveloped the game was. Nowadays, players go from town to town, country to country and challenge to challenge in super leagues.'

Although the financial rewards are substantial for the leading players, Croft denies that vast amounts are earned by every professional player. 'It is really only the select top few who make such handsome livings from darts. Lowe, Bristow, Wilson, perhaps Deller in the future—there are not many others in the big money league. And those that do make good money have to work very hard for it. There is no home life at all and they have to be totally dedicated to what they are doing.'

The BDO runs an international ranking list for British players. Points are earned from success in various events. Around sixteen tournaments are eligible for providing world ranking points to the players.

The world body is the World Darts Federation formed in 1976 at the instigation of the BDO, who by this time had established darts as a spectator sport. It is truly a cosmopolitan body and the general secretary is Olly Croft. The president is from New Zealand, the vice president is from Australia, the treasurer is American, and the co-ordinator a Welshman. Meetings are held once a year in a variety of venues.

Rules

One of the attractions of darts is its simplicity. It can be played alone, in a confined space, indoors (in any room). Besides, the rules and the scoring are easy to understand. The fans are closer to their heroes than followers of most sports, which create highly paid superstars who become remote from their origins.

Individual leagues and tournaments sometimes have their own rules but, broadly speaking, they follow a traditional pattern. The greatest difference between tournaments is likely to involve the mark line, known as the 'oche' or hockey where throwers must stand while aiming for the board. Some use the 7ft line; others increase the distance to anything up to 8ft. In rare cases, longer distances may be thrown but the 7ft to 8ft region is the accepted norm.

The 'official' distance was standardised at 7ft 9¼in by the BDO in 1977. This was a compromise between the 7ft 6in minimum approved by the NDA in 1954 and the 8ft distance common in other parts of the world. (In South Africa the traditional distance is 9ft).

The origin of the term 'oche' is obscure: the general view is that it is an old English word meaning the groove from which archers shot in competition; some believe that 'oche' is an old French word meaning nick or notch. But the archers' groove is the preferred derivation.

Only three darts may be used by a player and, to count as a score, the dart must be embedded in the board within the confines of the scoring segments or 'beds'. Darts which fall to the floor, usually after hitting a metal wire and being rejected, do not count.

The height of the dartboard from the floor is not of paramount importance in amateur contests. But in serious competition, it is accurately set at 5ft 8in from the centre of the bull to to the floor, with the number 20 segment always square to the top.

Various games can be played on a dartboard and it is the choice of the individuals concerned. The lowest game score is normally 201, the highest 1,001, with 501 the accepted target in most professional tournaments. The winner is the one who reduces his score to exactly nought and the dart which achieves this must land in a double. (The bull counts as double 25) If a player's score when the running total is subtracted would be one or less than zero, the turn is over—it is called 'busting'—and the score reverts to the number remaining before the opponent's last throw.

Most games are begun by throwing a double, although professional events tend to allow scores to count from the first throw. Amateurs often prefer the 'double-to-start' system but the professionals and amateur enthusiasts come together in their method of ending a game. That is always achieved by throwing a double.

In competitions, mathematical errors in calculating the score are rendered virtually impossible by modern technology. But in pub league games or amateur tournaments— where it was once traditional for a blackboard and chalk to be supplied for scoring—mistakes can sometimes occur in assessing a total. If this happens, the rules insist that mistakes must be pointed out immediately; they cannot be rectified afterwards, when other players have thrown.

Finishing: amateurs and professionals may differ in how they start a game of darts, a finish is always achieved by throwing a double. It is vital to be able to throw doubles and also to know all the going out combinations (which are listed in the statistics section at the end of the book, pages 60 and 61).

Definition of a dart

In 1980 the British Darts Organisation defined the dart as follows: A dart
1. Must not be more than 12in in length
2. Must not weigh more than 50g
3. Shall consist of a needle-type point which must be rigidly fixed to the barrel
4. Shall include a flighted stem which should consist of up to two pieces i.e. flight and stem

The declaration did not outlaw the spring-loaded dart which had caused so much of a rumpus. Some competitors claimed it gave others an unfair advantage but the strict regulations laid down ensured a standard dart. However, Keith Deller's victory in the 1983 world professional championships revived some of that controversy.

Spring-loaded darts

The advantage of the spring-loaded dart is said to be that it does not bounce out of the board as easily as the conventional dart. That can be absolutely vital for top professional players aiming at the narrow bed which offers darts' highest score—three triple 20s (180). Squeezing all three darts into the narrow space is a tricky affair; anything which helps may be of advantage, however slight.

Throwing distance: this was standardised by the BDO at 7ft 9¼in in 1977. But the throwing distances vary all over the world, wherever darts is played. In South Africa, for instance, a 9ft mark is common and before the BDO's 1977 ruling the standard distance was 7ft 6in, established by the National Darts Association in 1954.

5ft 8in

7ft 9¼in

The oche: this is the mark the players throw from.

Terminology

Although rules and scoring are straightforward darts has evolved quaint terms and strange sounding phrases. Busting with half-a-crown (throwing 26 which is more than the score remaining beside a player's name) or throwing a bag o'nuts (45) are terms still very much in use in the modern game, especially at pub and local league level. This darts dictionary includes many terms and here are a few examples.

Annie's room double one
Arrows darts
Away scoring a double to start a game
Bag o'nuts forty-five
Barrel the weighted section of a dart

Basement double three

Bed any scoring segment of the board but especially the doubles or trebles areas
Bed and Breakfast twenty-six total scored from 20, 5 and 1
Big Ben ten
Bombers extremely heavy darts

Brush failing to hit a double to start a match when your opponent has finished

Bull/Bung/Button centre ring, worth fifty
Bust(ing) scoring more than required and reverting to previous score
Cane darts shaft, formerly made of bamboo or rattan
Cannons another term for bombers
Chalk to keep the score
Clock (board) national competition board
Come out! call to a player who has scored too many

Cracked when a single of a number is scored instead of the attempted double

Double-in starting a game on a double
Double-out finishing a game on a double

Double Nelson a score of 222
Double top double twenty
Downstairs the lower half of the board
Elm wood used for dartboards
Feathers turkey feathers still used for some darts flights; also means thirty-three scored
Fish shop a score of twenty-two

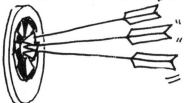

Game on! a call for quiet at the start of play
Game shot the winning double
Getting out making a game shot
Going bust scoring too many

Good arrows! term of congratulation for good throw

Half-a-crown a score of twenty-six, taken from pre-decimal coinage
Hitting the woodwork a shot off the board completely
Hockey or Oche the throwing line.

Island scoring surface of the dartboard
Killer a game played with darts for practice
Leg each game of several in a match

Leg and leg both players or teams have won one leg

Level pegging evenly matched game

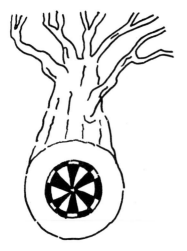

Nails extremely thin darts virtually the same width all the way down
No score all three darts outside the scoring wire or the number scored exceeds number required

Log-end old term for dartboard still used in Manchester area

Oche the throwing line (an Anglo Saxon word meaning a groove in the ground)

Off another term for 'away'

Lord Nelson a score of 111

Madhouse double one
Married man's side the left-hand side of the board, ie the safe side avoiding very low (and high) scores
Middle for diddle throwing for bull to start a game
Mugs away! loser of last game to start first in next game

One foot (or toe) in the water overstepping the oche

Oxo a score of nil; also the name of a darts game played on a standard board
Pug expression for bull

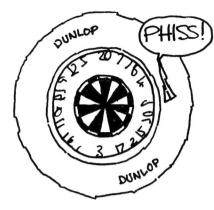

Puncture hitting the tyre, if there is one, around the board

Quadrant segment of the board composed of two adjacent numbers

Rankings official list of top players in the world

Rip scoring more than required

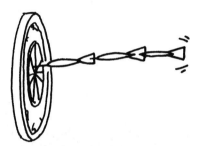

Robin Hood impaling a dart on the flight of a dart already in the board

Shafts formerly called canes, they screw into the end of the barrel to hold the flight—now made of fibreglass, aluminium, plastic, nylon or titanium

Shanghai scoring a single, double and treble on the same number with three darts

Shot out scoring the finishing double

Split an uneven number left

Stance the way a player stands on the oche

Strike a player throwing first in a leg is said to have the strike

Sunset Strip seventy-seven

Switching giving up one number and aiming for another

Three in a bed three darts landed in the same bed

Tin hat to be brushed

Ton a score of one hundred

Tops/Top of the house (or shop) double twenty

Tungsten metal with high specific gravity now used extensively for dart barrels

Turf another term for island

Turf Moor No 4

Umbrellas seventy-seven

Upstairs the upper section of the board

Varieties fifty-seven (courtesy of Heinz)

Wet feet overstepping the oche

Whitewash failing to hit a starting double before opponent finishes a game

Win the toss, lose the game darts proverb

Wiring one bouncing the dart off the wire or landing it next to the wire

Wrong bed dart falling in the wrong number

15

The Stars

Eric Bristow

Eric Bristow is the unofficial world number one. But this cheerful, ebullient Cockney character failed to land darts' biggest tournament, the Embassy world professional championship, in both 1982 and 1983. Bristow bounced back quickly after his shock defeat in the 1983 final to an unknown—Keith Deller—by winning the British Open. He avenged the defeat by beating Deller 6–2 in a £10,000 challenge sponsored by the Isle of Man tourist board and shown on BBC *Grandstand*. This was the highest individual prize.

Jocky Wilson in 1982 and Deller in 1983 denied Bristow world titles he seemed destined to collect. So the man who won the world title in 1980 and 1981 to become undisputed world number one, has a struggle to retain his status.

Bristow has been landing major titles since he clinched the 1977 world masters which he also won again in 1979 and 1981. He was British open champion in 1978, 1981 and 1983 and runner-up in 1982. In April 1983 he realised a lifelong ambition by winning the *News of the World* trophy, beating Ralph Flatt in the final without conceding a leg and scoring three

Eric Bristow
Born: 25 April 1957.
Right-handed. Single.
Lives in Stoke-on-Trent
Previous jobs: Salesman in furniture store, proof-reader, plasterer's mate.
Best performance: World professional champion, 1980 and 1981.

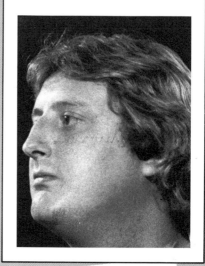

16

Eric Bristow

180s.

When Bristow lost the 1983 world professional final to Deller, he was still only 25-years-old. That underlines his astonishing progress in the early years of a career which has made him the top darts name in the world.

Bristow, an East Londoner, who is nicknamed the Crafty Cockney, has a distinctive playing style. He throws with his fifth finger up in the air—'me perked-up right pinky' as he calls it. His style, his bold prophecies and his excellent results have made him the sort of character fans love to hate.

Bristow is not worried by his detractors: 'I suppose I'm in a situation where some people will want to knock me. But, to be honest, I've got too much to do, too many commitments in the world of darts to sit around being concerned at that. When I finally retire from darts, I would like to leave the sort of record that future champions are always struggling to match. Great

players from other sports have done much the same thing and that's what I would like to achieve in darts.'

Already his financial earnings from the sport are in excess of £100,000 each year. But Bristow works hard, touring the exhibition halls up to four or five nights a week and travelling abroad many times a year for more exhibitions, tournaments and special tours.

Bristow may exude brash confidence—that is part of his style. But he is enough of a realist to know that British players, until now regarded as the finest in the world, are set to face a stiff battle to retain supremacy.

Bristow has not gone out of his way to cultivate the Cockney character image but he has done little to dispel its development. 'I have always been a cheeky little what-name,' he jokes. 'Anyway, that's the way I am. People can take me or leave me as they please.'

John Lowe

One of the steadiest, most consistent and conservative players currently on the world scene is Derbyshire's John Lowe. He presents the quiet, unobtrusive image which contrasts with Bristow's brash Cockney appeal and Wilson's often controversial manner.

Lowe was world professional champion in 1979, runner-up in 1981 to Bristow and in 1982 to Jocky Wilson. He has won most of darts' greatest prizes in his career, including the world masters title in 1976 and 1980 and is one of darts' top money-earners of all time.

Rated number one in England before Bristow burst onto the scene, he slipped down to number four at the end of the 1970s as fatigue caught up with him. But Lowe recovered his appetite for the game in 1981–2 and became again one of the toughest men to beat, although tournament wins have been limited in the last two years. England captain, and deservedly so, he offers a popular appeal as the 'gentleman' of the darts world.

John Lowe
Born: 21 July 1945.
Right-handed. Married.
Lives in Chesterfield,
Derbyshire.
Previous job: Joiner.
Hobbies: Golf, gardening, motor sports.
Best performance: World professional champion, 1979.

The Stars/3

Jocky Wilson

His greatest achievement was victory in the 1982 world professional tournament which made him world number one. He beat John Lowe in the final to secure his greatest prize, but after that slipped back and could not repeat his success in the 1983 event, losing to the eventual winner, Keith Deller, in the semi-finals.

Wilson has been Scotland's number one for several years and was a solid, consistent winner in 1980–2. He was BBC television's 'Bullseye' champion in 1980 and 1981, British open champion in 1982, Unipart British professional champion in 1981, Holsten matchplay champion the same year and Ladbroke matchplay champion in 1980. He has come closest to achieving a nine-dart finish on TV.

He got into serious trouble for attacking an official in a tournament in 1982. He was fined £1,000 and banned from representing his country by the SDA (Scottish Darts Association). But the BDO did not recognise the ban because they claimed it was not handled in the proper manner.

Wilson missed the 1983 Nations Cup tournament. His problems may have stemmed from the fact that drink is synonymous with darts. Wilson suffers from tension and found drink helped to reduce nerves. He used to drink pints of beer but turned to spirits and this began to affect, not aid, his game so he cut down his intake.

When the problems started—culminating in bad behaviour at various functions—Wilson's reputation suffered. Happily, he has started to overcome those problems and should climb back to the top as a player in the years to come.

He is a tigerish competitor, capable of beating all-comers. Effervescent, sometimes unpredictable, his squat frame makes him instantly recognisable on the circuit.

Jocky Wilson
Born: 22 March 1950.
Right-handed. Married with three children.
Lives it Kirkcaldy, Fife.
Previous jobs: miner, factory worker.
Best performance: World Professional champion, 1982.

Alan Evans

This chirpy Welshman was born in the Rhondda Valley but now lives in Stockport and plays county darts for Lancashire. He started darts at six-years-old in his father's pub and was runner-up in the 1972 *News of the World* event. His best year was in 1975 when he won the world masters and British open titles.

Evans captained Wales when they won the world cup in 1972. He often partners Leighton Rees and they won the Danish pairs title in 1978. The following year he was banned by the Welsh Darts Organisation because of an incident after the home internationals.

Alan Evans

Born: 14 June 1949.
Right-handed. Married.
Job: Contracts manager in an engineering firm.
Hobbies: Manchester City FC.
Best performance: World masters and British open titles, 1975.

The Stars/4

Tony Brown

A full England international and ranked number three in the world in 1981 behind Bristow and Lowe, Brown is a steady, consistent thrower from Dover, Kent. He has not quite climbed the final couple of rungs on the ladder to reach the top slot.

He was British open champion in 1979, European singles champion in 1981 and World Cup pairs champion, 1981. He was a member of England's winning World Cup team at Las Vegas in 1979 and Nelson, New Zealand in 1981.

He may have reached the zenith of his achievements but is still capable of consistent earning on the exhibition circuit, which is always a busy and profitable area of the darts world.

Tony Brown
Born: 1 April 1945.
Right-handed. Married with four children—all girls.
Lives in Dover,
Previous job: Manager in paper mill.
Hobbies include reading and record-collecting.

Cliff Lazarenko

Ranked number four in the world in 1981 and 1982—his highest ever position—Lazarenko was another member of England's winning World Cup team in New Zealand in 1981. His other titles that year included the Danish Open and World Cup pairs championship.

He was British Open champion in 1980, his greatest success. Still a popular competitor on the circuit, he has the ability to beat the best in the world.

Although his peak form has often been too much for the top men, he tends to fall away when well poised for victory. Inconsistency has frequently been a problem. A big man at 6ft 4in and 20 stone.

Cliff Lazarenko
Born: 16 March 1952.
Right-handed. Married.
Lives in Northampton.
Previous job: Construction worker.
Hobbies: Snooker and football.
Best performance: British Open champion, 1980.

Tony Brown

Cliff Lazarenko

The Stars/5

Dave Whitcombe

A steadily improving young player from Kent, Whitcombe was *News of the World* runner-up in 1980 and Marlboro Masters champion in 1980, the year before he won tournaments at Butlins and Pontins to boost his reputation.

His best performance was in 1982 when he won the Winmau world masters title to confirm beliefs that he was continuing to make progress. His best position in the world rankings was sixth in 1983 but, with further improvement, he could climb again in the top echelons of the game.

Stefan Lord

Sweden's number one darts player for several years, Lord has now earned the right to be called the best non-British player in the world. He fell away in the early 1980s after a bright start in this country when he became *News of the World* champion in 1978 and 1980. But the Swede came back to form in 1982 and 1983, deserving a ranking well inside the top ten in the world.

Dave Whitcombe
Born: 27 June 1954.
Right-handed. Single.
Home town: Clacton, Essex.
Previous job: electrician.
Hobbies: chess, photography, boxing and snooker.
Best performance: World Masters winner, 1982.

Stefan Lord
Born: Sweden, 4 December 1954.
Right-handed.
Hobbies: Ice hockey.
Best performance: *News of the World* champion, 1978 and 1980.

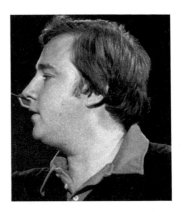

Dave Whitcombe

Stefan Lord

The Stars/6

Bobby George
At one time, this flamboyant character with his eye-catching clothes was rated number three in the world. But a severe illness because of a damaged spleen in October 1980 almost ended not only his career but his life.

He has gradually recovered, without quite finding the form which once made him such a superlative player. He won the European Cup singles but disappointed in other major tournaments in 1982 and did little in the 1983 world championship. However, he is a popular man on the exhibition circuit becase of the great character he is.

Nicky Virachkul
Virachkul went to live in the United States in 1968 and is now the American number one but has slipped out of the top ten in the world ratings. He was World Cup singles champion in 1979—his best victory—and won the North American open in 1982.

He has been on the fringe of the very top ranks ever since. But his erratic form has prevented him from reaching the peak. But he remains popular throughout the world, especially in the United States and in his native Thailand where his exploits are closely followed. Another player who had the chance of a televised 9 dart finish. He threw for a double-12 with his 9th dart.

Bobby George
Born: 16 December 1945.
Right-handed. Married.
Home town: Ilford, Essex.
Previous job: Floor laying
Hobbies: Fishing
Best performance: European Cup singles, 1982.

Nicky Virachkul
Born: Thailand, 3 June 1948.
Right-handed.
Lives in Dallas, Texas.
Hobbies: reading and golf.
Best performance: World Cup singles champion, 1979.

Bobby George

Nicky Virachkul

Steve Brennan

He was New Zealand open champion in 1981, has been Northern Ireland's captain and was rated between twelfth and fifteenth in the world in 1981–2.

He remains most famous for his astonishing first round victory over Eric Bristow, the defending champion, in the 1982 world championship. That win catapulted Brennan into the headlines but he has been unable to build upon that fine victory. Since then, results have been something of a disappointment, although his decision to devote more time to his game could prove beneficial.

Leighton Rees

Leighton was one of the most famous names in darts in the 1970s but has slipped back from that level. He captained Wales in many international tournaments and remains a fine ambassador for his country. He still lives in his home village Ynysybwl in Glamorgan and is the most capped international player.

He became world professional champion in 1978, probably the height of his achievements. At his peak, he was rated number two in the world but has fallen from that lofty perch, and has lost his place as Welsh number one to Ceri Morgan.

Steve Brennan
Born: 2 November 1951.
Right-handed. Married.
Lives in Leiston, Suffolk.
Previous job: Supervisor in civil engineering firm.
Hobbies: Golf and snooker.
Best performance: New Zealand Open Champion, 1981.

Leighton Rees
Born: 17 January 1940.
Right-handed.
Lives at Ynysybwl, Glamorgan.
Previous job: Storeman.
Hobbies: Swimming and rugby.
Best performance: World Professional champion, 1978.

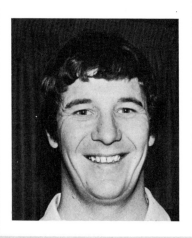

Leighton Rees

Steve Brennan

29

The Stars/8

Ceri Morgan

Ceri is the Welsh number one although he has yet to fulfil his potential. He made his first appearance for Wales in 1974. He seemed to have the ability to live with the best but has never produced that form consistently enough to win a major title.

He keeps busy as an exhibition player but must feel, like many of his colleagues in the top darts league, that he ought to be beating the big names and landing famous trophies. In all events he is very much a dark horse, capable of producing an upset.

Ceri Morgan
Born: 22 December 1947.
Right-handed. Single.
Home: Glamorgan.
No previous job.
Hobbies: Pub crawling.
Best performance: British Masters champion, 1980.

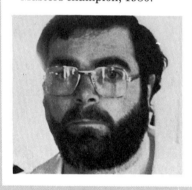

Luc Marreel

The Belgian number one, Marreel was regarded as a potential candidate for the top ten in darts rating league. He failed to justify that optimism in 1982 but retains the unpredictable ability which could take him far closer to the top. He is a busy player in his own country as well as on the international circuit.

Luc Marreel
Born: 5 February 1949.
Right-handed. Married.
Home town: Hullegem, Belgium.
Previous job: Docker.
Hobbies: Pigeons.

30

Ceri Morgan

Terry O'Dea

The 6ft 2in, 17 stone Australian took up darts in 1965 after injuring a knee playing Australian Rules Football. Married with three girls, he manages a hotel in Perth, Western Australia.

Although he claims to play and practise less than most professionals—he plays twice a week and practises once a week—he has won Australian singles and doubles titles and represented his country in the 1979 world cup. Now a familiar figure in Britain, his ambition is to win a major title in this country. His best effort was to reach the quarter finals of the world championships.

Terry O'Dea
Born: 3 May 1945.
Right-handed. Married.
Job: Hotel manager.
Hobbies: Golf, Australian rules football.

31

Alan Glazier

One of the first professionals, Glazier is known as the 'best runner-up in the business'. He has reached the final of most top events—including the British open, the British matchplay and the *News of the World*. But his only big win was in the 1980 Embassy Licensed Victuallers event. For many years the leading left-handed player, Glazier is now being pressed for that distinction by Scotland's Peter Masson.

Paul Lim

Singapore's number one, he, like Marreel, has not fulfilled what seemed to be a great natural promise. He burst onto the world scene in 1980 by winning the Pacific Cup and was apparently ready to challenge Stefan Lord's unofficial claim to the number one international player slot, outside the United Kingdom. But despite a heavy schedule which sees him playing in many parts of the world, he has not yet turned potential into success.

Alan Glazier
Born: 21 January 1939.
Left-handed. Single.
Home town: London. Lives in Cambridge.
Best performance: Winner Embassy LV title, 1980

Paul Lim
Born: 25 January 1954.
Right-handed. Single.
Home town: Singapore.
Previous job: Chef.
Hobbies: Fishing and diving.
Best performance: Pacific Cup winner 1980.

Alan Glazier

33

The Stars/10

Maureen Flowers

Maureen is the girlfriend of Eric Bristow and a suitable match for the world number one in more ways than one! She is regarded as the best woman player in the world, ranked number one by the British Darts Organisation.

She was champion in the British open women's singles in 1982 and also won the women's pairs in that tournament, together with Linda Batten. She has had success all around the world on the tournament scene, as shown by victories in the North American open in 1977, 1979 and 1981; the Danish championship and Swedish championship both in 1981. She is a regular England international.

Women's darts are generally not recognised to the same extent as the men's game and for Maureen Flowers that is a pity. She is far and away the leading light in the ladies' game.

Linda Batten

Regarded as number two to Maureen Flowers in the women's rankings for some years, she has become a steady, consistent player who has won many titles at home and abroad. She was British open champion in 1980 but since then has slipped back a little and that number two ranking has definitely been under challenge from several quarters. She has been a full England international for many years.

Linda has been instrumental in the sudden emergence of Keith Deller as men's world champion. Apart from helping Deller in practice in the run-up to his world championship win in 1983, she is the greatest influence on his career—by his own reckoning. Her ambition is to captain England and become the number one woman in darts.

Maureen Flowers
Born: 6 December 1946.
Right-handed. Separated.
Best performance: British women's champion, 1982.

Linda Batten
Born: 1955.
Right-handed. Single.
Hobbies: walking dogs, ballet and opera.
Best performance: British women's champion, 1980

Anne-Marie Davies

The blonde mother of a four-year-old boy, Anne-Marie hails from Tonypandy in the Rhondda Valley where she still lives. Her first big win was the British women's title in 1982 and she followed that up by becoming the first ever women's world champion in 1983.

Anne-Marie Davies
Born: 30 April 1959.
Right handed. Divorced.
Home: Tonypandy.
Hobbies: Tennis, pool, snooker.
Best performance: Women's world champion, 1983.

Linda Batten wins.

Maureen Flowers

35

Road to the top

There is an old joke in the musical profession.

'How do you get to Carnegie Hall?' asks the young man, guitar in hand.

'Practise, man, practise' is the reply.

Leading darts players, who have become household names, will accompany their chuckle with a knowing nod. The story is the same in darts, as in most sports. Most top class sportsmen will talk at length of the need to practise constantly. Even competitors of rich, natural ability—such as snooker's Alex 'Hurricane' Higgins and the inimitable Manchester United and Northern Ireland soccer star George Best—honed their skills on the practice ground, through long, often laborious sessions.

Standing on the 'oche' under the television lights—with your throw at a dart-board a few feet away seen in millions of homes—is the ultimate achievement on the darts ladder. Climbing that ladder is not nearly as straightforward as many would imagine.

Perfecting any technique cannot be achieved overnight. Darts players like Bristow, Deller, Lowe and Wilson talk of hours of daylight, stretching into the night, throwing darts at a practice board. In darts, the dividing line between success and failure is comparatively slim; minute measurements separate a triple twenty from a single one or five. So practice is imperative. Concentration and strong nerves are also essential under the intense pressure of matchplay darts for big prizes under the glare of the television lights.

Concentrating the aim on that tiny 'bed' on the board which offers the lucrative prize of 180 (from three darts of triple twenty) requires not only skill but dedication to practice bordering on the fanatical. That such practice and dedication to the game bring rewards is illustrated by the startling arrival

Road to the top/2

upon the professional scene of a young man like Deller.

Where does it all begin? Young players can start on the competitive ladder at an early age. The British teenage championships cover youngsters competing in the 13 to 18 age group. These championships coincide with the finish of the county season in July and August. The tournament is run through various counties with play-offs at county level. Junior events are also held at places such as holiday camps, some for players aged just 11 or 12.

All the leading players in the professional ranks began as amateurs. The National Darts Association of Great Britain (NDAGB) runs ten individual national championships, often with as many as 12–15,000 people taking part. Some may be the Bristows or the Dellers of tomorrow's professional world; all will be taking their first, tentative steps on the ladder towards the top. Entries for NDAGB events come from all over the British Isles and the Republic of Ireland.

Playing the game to a useful standard at pub level is another step on the road to the top. Matches are arranged between rival pubs and more serious games are run by county associations. From that standard, national tournaments may be within the reach of the better players and on that rostrum is the opportunity to strike out for the top against some of the best known names in the game.

Few of the top professionals forget one other aspect of their success: the one-night stands, or exhibition matches which provide them with a twofold advantage. Exhibition nights feature a top name player being invited to a pub or club or special venue to challenge local champions or pub competitors.

The pay provides players with a steady income: Jocky Wilson earned

Keeping score: a packed crowd watches a Wales v England match in 1983. Inset, organised events have scorers such as these ladies to keep tally.

38

Road to the top/3

£20,000 from the Strongbow Cider Company for a series of exhibition matches. Marlboro sponsored a team of champions—Lowe, Brown, Smith, Rees and Baker, with each player earning a lucrative fee. John Lowe made £18,000 to £20,000 for a series of exhibition sponsorships over the course of a year.

Leighton Rees and Bobby George earned £1,000 for a week playing to British soldiers in West Germany. Exhibitions, for the top individual players, are worth £400 to £500 a night, although they are becoming fewer. Many exhibition halls and centres now prefer to take a lesser known star and use him, perhaps at a fee of £150 a night, rather than spend more money on a John Lowe or Eric Bristow.

Exhibitions also provide invaluable practice under matchplay conditions and help the professional prepare for the special demands of pressure play. Players smile at the determination of locals, resolved to topple a famous player in an exhibition. But they are good for the professional, good for the amateurs, and above all, good for darts.

However, riding the exhibition circuit, as it is known in the trade, is a gruelling, unrelenting affair. Manchester one night, Birmingham the next; perhaps Southampton the one after and Brighton the night after that. Many players take on four or, in some cases, five nights a week at exhibition matches but the players' determination, not to say stamina, is sorely tested. The travelling is the toughest part—driving through the night, in some instances, after exhibition events in the evening to make progress on the journey to the following night's venue.

Eric Bristow chose carefully the siting of his home when he bought a house in Stoke-on-Trent. 'I had to have somewhere within reach of all the Northern clubs where I do so many exhibition matches. But I also needed somewhere near the Midlands because there is a lot of work there. And the house had to be very close to a motorway—to reach London and the south with comparative ease.'

Unlike most sports, darts does not require sheer physical fitness and strenuous exercise. Indeed, it veers towards the other extreme with many of the players admitting a weight problem. The reason is obvious: too little time for proper exercise; too much time spent sitting in cars on the move or standing around in clubs or pubs. There is the additional factor of alcohol, which many players take to calm taut nerves before and during contests.

Of course, the setting for the game of darts lends itself to the consumption of drink which is close at hand and needed by players working in often hot, overcrowded conditions. Hence the growing need for top professionals to employ chauffeurs to drive them from event to event.

Darts may seem to offer great reward for little effort. The truth is very different. The game requires immense dedication, fierce concentration and infinite practice to reach the top and stay there.

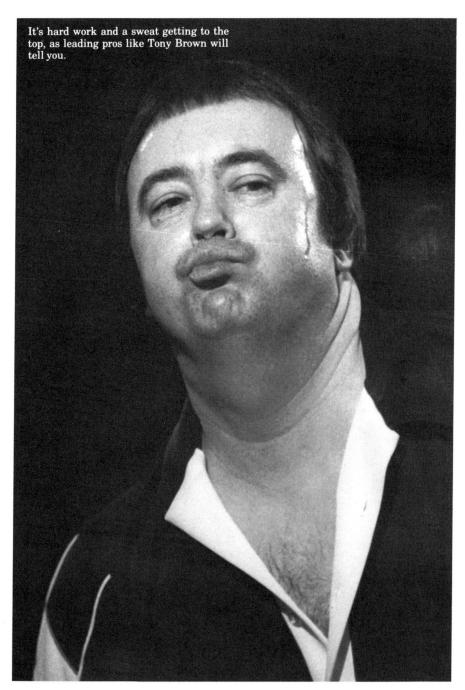

It's hard work and a sweat getting to the top, as leading pros like Tony Brown will tell you.

Road to the top/4

Deller's route to the top was the traditional, well-trodden path, through long, lonely hours of practice. He honed his technique at home and on countless evenings at his local pub, the Rising Sun in Whetstone, North London where he played regularly for many years.

He caused one of the biggest sensations in darts history when he shot from nowhere into the World Professional championship winner's shirt at the start of 1983. To defeat players of the calibre of John Lowe, Jocky Wilson and, in the final, Eric Bristow, proved Deller has a rich, natural talent which had blossomed and reached fruition in one competition. The 23-year-old from Ipswich may have surprised almost the entire darts world by winning the world's premier title. But he did not surprise himself.

'I had been winning tournaments for so long that I knew I would get the title sooner or later if everything went right on the day. You get used to the idea of being a winner, that is the important thing. And I hope to earn some good money from the game. That is very much part of the attraction.'

Deller's list of titles in 1981 illustrated the universal appeal of darts. He was Hastings open champion; Texas open champion; Cleveland, Ohio, open champion and Suffolk open champion, all in that year. In 1982 he won the Benson and Hedges Hamlet pairs title with Steve Brennan and victory in the Los Angeles singles qualified him for the Embassy.

In certain respects, Deller is similar in character to Bristow. He is not reluctant to mention his achievements, or to outline his ambitions and attributes. But he is a slimline star, unlike Bristow and the other top players, who fit uneasily into conventional clothes.

Deller does not match the image of leading darts players in other ways. For a start, he does not drink much. 'I get a little nervous before a match but once I get up to the board, I'm perfectly all right. I can control my nerves,' he says confidently.

He did not win the world professional championship title by chance but after hours, days, months and years of solid, grinding practice, starting in the kitchen under the eagle eyes of his dart-devoted parents. It would have driven less committed young men to despair—or drink! That kind of immense concentration and determination to succeed stood him in good stead for the big championships.

The hours spent alone perfecting the art of accurate throwing was sufficient to turn him into a machine and he hit the big scores with astonishing regularity. In 1980–81, he started to get help and practice sessions with Linda Batten, who arranged a free trip to America, where he won $6,000. Linda and Keith have been known to practise for five hours and then play a match to decide who would cook supper.

The future holds much for Deller if he can match his entry into the top flight and he is set to join that exclusive set earning over £100,000 a year from darts—along with Bristow, Lowe and Wilson.

He is single and very popular with the female fans. In 1983 he took delivery of a new Mercedes which was part of an endorsement deal and had more than 150 exhibition matches lined up for 1983 at around £250 per night. He signed a brewery sponsorship deal with Ind Coop worth £50,000—the biggest individual sponsorship in the game's history involving fifty exhibition matches against customers at clubs and pubs. Clothing firms are eager to sign him up to promote their fashions.

A supporter of Ipswich Town, Deller was delighted to show off his Embassy trophy in front of the football fans at Portman Road. 'It was perhaps the next best thing that could happen to me . . . next to playing for Ipswich Town,' Deller told *Darts World* Magazine.

Keith Deller
Born: 24 December 1960
Right-handed. Single.
Home team: Ipswich
Hobbies: Pool, tennis and football
Previous job: Bakery worker

Events and competitions

The lengthening list of events reflects the growing interest of sponsors in a game which offers so many attractions, to players and spectators alike. As darts grow in esteem major companies vie for promotional interests, wishing to be associated with a game generally devoid of unsavoury aspects such as football hooliganism, despite the fact that darts is so clearly associated with alcohol.

The major event in the darts year is unquestionably the Embassy World professional championships, a jamboree to decide the man entitled to wear the mantle of world champion for the next twelve months. But if the tournament remains the number one on the calendar, that is not to say that the many other competitions are not of vital importance to individuals and countries. For many years, the *News of the World* was the number one tournament in many players' eyes and it retains the aura and importance which has kept it going ever since 1928, the war years excepted.

Each event gives players the chance to earn points towards world and British ranking positions. But the handsome cash prizes and prestige are also a major spur. Through exhibition matches, it is possible for a player to earn a good living from the game without winning *any* tournaments. But to earn the highest exhibition fees, top players must prove themselves regular winners on the circuit. So the tournaments which are staged regularly throughout the year hold great importance.

The Berger Brolac British open championships attract the top UK players, as illustrated by the list of past winners which include Jocky Wilson and Eric Bristow. It is played over two days, usually in January. The Unipart British professional championships is another event the leading players aim for. The Unipart event is by invitation only, to the top thirty-two professionals, and it lasts eight days—usually in September.

In 1981, Wilson picked up a cheque for £6,000 for winning the Unipart but his World professional championship success the following year—although probably greater in prestige and thus holding immense potential for future earnings—gave him a prize of £6,500, only £500 more. The British open—which used to be sponsored by Watney—carries a first prize of £3,000 with the runner-up collecting £1,000.

Women players participating in events such as the British open do not earn such big prizes. Maureen Flowers' victory in 1982 gave her a £1,000 prize with the runner-up, Pam Bailey, earning £500. By contrast the men's pairs in the same championships yielded the winners—Eric Bristow and John Lowe—a £1,000 cheque to split; the women's pairs winners, Maureen Flowers and Linda Batten, shared £500.

Other leading events and competitions include the Embassy licensed victuallers tournament, which follows the Embassy world professional championships and is the biggest charity fund-raising tournament on the darts calendar. Joe Dodd, from Buckinghamshire, won the 1982 tournament to collect a £1,000 prize plus a holiday worth £500.

The Winmau World masters, Dunlop masters, the Butlins grand masters, the Austin Morris British masters, the Dry Blackthorn masters and Berger Brolac British open championships are marginally less important. But the prize money ensures a first class entry list. Eric Bristow's victory in the 1981 Austin Morris British masters earned him a brand new Princess saloon car worth £5,500; he also picked up the first prize that year in the Watney tournament of £3,000.

The major team event on the world circuit is the World cup, dominated for many years by the strong English team. With players like Eric Bristow, John Lowe, Bobby George and Tony Brown to select from, it was not surprising to see the English team dominant in many world cups. Other team tournaments include the Europe cup—which is held every other year and scheduled for the Netherlands in 1984—and the nations cup.

But it is not only the major tournaments that attract the top players.

Lowe, for example, won the 1981 Nottingham open, underlining the point that the stars still play the smaller events, which offer tournament level competition to all players. The Dunlop masters includes extensive heats which determine county selection winners, and the BDO runs an intercounties championship which is open to many average pub players. Events of all shapes and sizes, open to all standards of players, give the darts world, professional and amateur, healthy competition.

The first major competition was the *News of the World,* started in 1928 and still going strong. This shows a pre-war event at the Palais de Danse in Ilford with the competition's signature tune of the day.

Clubs

A new development is threatening the traditional link between professional darts and the major clubs of the north where the game has developed. Clubs such as Jollees, in Stoke-on-Trent, and the Fiesta Club, Stockton, have altered their traditional mode of business to concentrate on discos. Hence, these famous old stamping grounds of the top stars may cease to be such familiar darts venues.

The clubs, especially in the north, have always provided a unique atmosphere for big darts events. It would clearly be a pity if the game lost that famous flavour because the excitement and feeling generated by the clubs is certainly a key ingredient of the game. The future link between the clubs and the game's major competitions is in doubt. If that doubt is confirmed, major tournaments could be held in future in halls such as Alexandra Palace ('Ally Pally') in North London, which staged the 1983 Nations cup, and the Rainbow Suite in Kensington.

Leading darts expert Tony Green says: 'Both venues have much to offer. But personally, I hope some way can be found to maintain those old links between the game and the clubs up north. Darts in those clubs seems somehow special and I believe the game would lose something if it were no longer staged in such familiar settings.'

The hum of excitement created by those clubs is completely different and very much part of the darts folklore. Betting is allowed inside the building—normally just outside the playing arena—and this adds to the enthusiasm from the audience which is seated around tables across a wide spectator area, quite close to the throwing area. Corals handle betting at the World professional championships; Ladbrokes take the British open and British professional tournaments.

The characters who turn up decked out in flags (if it is a national team event) or scarves favouring certain players contribute to the scene. Pints of beer and thick smoke are standard equipment—as important, it seems, as the darts themselves.

The favourite players attract special crowds and assorted encouragment, depending on their relationship with the supporters. Bristow invariably evokes loud comment, good and bad; Wilson, always a controversial character, has much the same effect; Lowe is a quieter person but retains a strong, loyal support.

In the London halls, the atmosphere seems to be diluted, whereas in the close confines of the clubs the audience provides a cacophony of sound which reverberates around the room. Halls are less personal and do not transmit that effect as easily.

Other popular venues include the Wembley Conference Centre; the Afan Lido, Aberavon; the Playhouse, Edinburgh, and the Sunderland Empire. These are the other well known provincial centres. Yet darts at the top professional level still retains a good following, whatever the venue.

It could be that its change from a traditional base around the clubs of the north to the slightly more sophisticated halls of the south will herald a fresh challenge to the game's continuing development. Darts, as a game, has changed in a variety of ways over the centuries. This latest innovation may be merely the next stage of that steady evolution.

But the story of venues in darts crosses all continents, for the game has spread throughout the world. Far from being an exclusive preserve of British northern clubs or public houses, matches are now staged in the most unlikely settings on unexpected continents.

Darts events attract big crowds both live and on television. Fans can become wrapped up in a match or as partisan as football supporters with all usual scarves and favours. There is no doubting which team is followed by these scarf-waving fans, but individual players also receive fervent, vocal backing (and abuse!).

Equipment

As the game has expanded, the manufacturing industries associated with it have grown. There is a back-up industry worth hundreds of thousands of pounds every year and the range of goods is now extensive.

The Dart

Perhaps the greatest development in a technical sense has been the modification of the dart itself. Darts featuring various metals including aluminium, tungsten and brass have come onto the market. Weights vary from heavy to super light-weight, depending on the individual's personal taste. Tungsten is denser than brass so darts can be made thinner, which helps grouping on the board.

Barrel and Shaft

While the barrel is metal, the shaft can be made of a variety of materials such as titanium, nylon, fibre-glass, aluminium or plastic. Shaft designs change constantly with new developments. Instant loading, built-in protector cap, high-flex strength all pertain to the shaft. Darts featuring nickel tungsten, polyester flights, revolutionary grip tips, anodised aluminium, self-adhesive flights and nylon shafts are available.

Shops stock large quantities of darts to suit all tastes. There are, at a conservative estimate, two hundred different types of barrel and over one hundred shafts to choose from. That figure is increasing all the time as the market caters for the growing demand.

Dart care

Care of darts is important. The top professionals often look after their darts themselves, making minor adjustments when required. Others will leave that task to a manager but any change in a favourite trio of darts will be thoroughly tested and examined

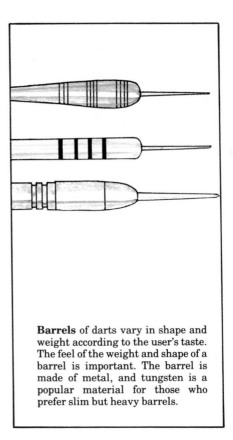

Barrels of darts vary in shape and weight according to the user's taste. The feel of the weight and shape of a barrel is important. The barrel is made of metal, and tungsten is a popular material for those who prefer slim but heavy barrels.

well before use in an important tournament.

The point of the dart should be kept sharp at all times. A tip which is slightly blunt may mean the difference between a triple twenty and rejection by the board when the tip makes contact. This may seem obvious and professionals are as fussy about their equipment as any top class sportsmen. But amateurs are not always so careful.

A dart sharpener similar to a pencil sharpener, can be acquired for about 40p. When the points wear down and affect the balance of the dart, it is possible—and often preferable—to replace the points rather than buy and get used to a new set.

48

Buyers' guide

The enormous range of darts can present a bewildering choice for beginners and for pub players. Tungsten darts (80/20 nickel or 90/10 nickel), in a variety of different weights to suit individual requirements, are the most popular.

When buying darts and accessories, it is advisable to visit one of the specialist shops around the country. Most of these have a couple of dartboards on the premises so that you can try many different types of darts to find ones that suit you. Leading darts centres in London include Frank Johnson's at 189 Ferndale Road, Brixton, SW9 (01–733 1722) and Gerry's of Wimbledon at 170–176 The Broadway, SW19 1RX (01–542 7792).

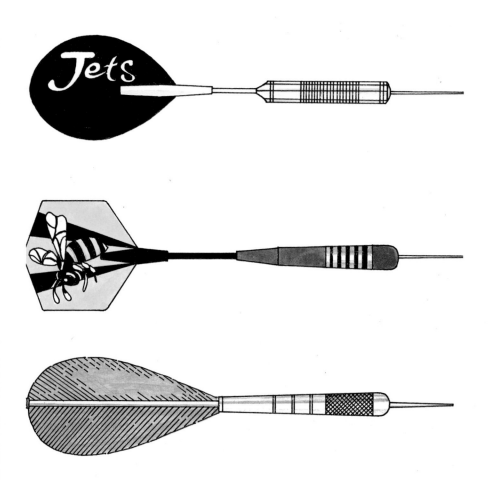

Equipment/2

Other darts stockists with a wide range of equipment are the Midlands Darts Centre, 68 Tividale Road, Tividale, Warley, West Midlands B69 2LQ (021–520 6999); Bullseye Darts Centre, 709 Abbeydale Road, Sheffield, South Yorkshire S7 2BE (0742–580150); E G and P R Norman, 453, Gloucester Road, Horfield, Bristol BS7 8TZ (0272–514415). Most of the shops have a mail order catalogue and can supply by post.

Prices vary considerably. Dartboards are made of three materials—paper, bristle and natural elm. Paper boards vary from £1 to £7; bristle boards cost from £13.95 to £16.95 and elm boards upwards of £17.50.

The best boards were always considered to be elm. But to keep an elm board in good condition, it is important to soak it in water perhaps three times a week. Boards which do not receive this treatment tend to dry out, making the wood susceptible to bending and uneven shape. Hence the growing popularity of bristle boards which tend to last longer.

A brass set of darts would cost from £2.30 to £5; tungsten darts cost from £10 to £25 a set. Brass darts are less popular because of their bulkiness. 'It is like throwing a bomb, throwing one of those things,' one leading stockist remarked. 'Tungsten darts are better becase you get the weight without the bulk of the brass darts.'

Tungsten darts are two and half times as heavy as brass darts, but they are thinner which makes it easier to group all three into a compact treble bed.

Unlike many others sports, darts requires no special dress. Clothing should be practical and comfortable—a loose-neck, short-sleeved shirt which in no way restricts arm-movement. Jackets are not worn because they are restrictive and thick sweaters are seldom seen.

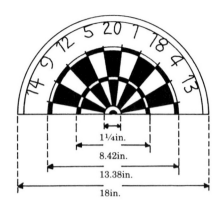

The London or International board is the one accepted in most top competitions these days. A Bury carpenter called Brian Gamlin is thought to be the man responsible for the arrangement of numbers in 1896. The order, clockwise from the top, is 20, 1, 18, 4, 13, 6, 10, 15, 2, 17, 3, 19, 7, 16, 8, 11, 14, 9, 12, 5.

Flights are often made of plastic or polyester and they carry all kinds of decoration from the manufacturers or sponsors name to a favourite football club.

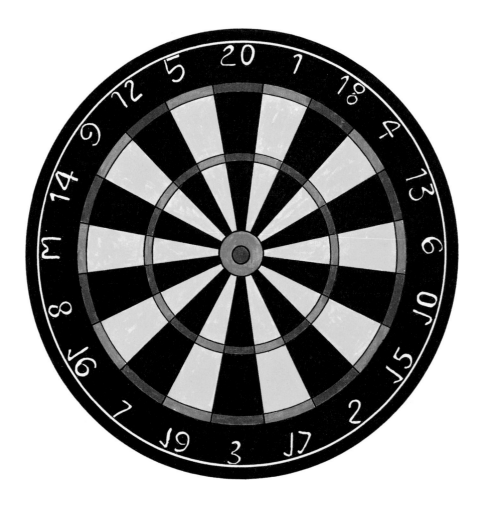

Dartboards were once simple log ends — and they are still referred to as such in certain areas. These days the best boards are made of elm, but they needed regular soaking in water if they are not to dry out and warp. So boards made of bristle or sisal fibres from East Africa are becoming increasingly popular. Plasticine and cork are also used. In bristle or sisal boards over 16 million fibres are used and the colours are screen-printed. The non-scoring area is usually black with the scoring sections alternately black and yellow (or black and white on cheaper boards). The better boards alternate between red and green colours for the double and triple beds.

The modern bristle boards are thought to cause less damage to the darts. To reduce wear and tear on well-used sections such as the 20, the numbers are turned round from time to time and many boards are also reversable. The numbers are bent into the wire (or painted on cheaper boards).

Equipment/3

The London or Standard or International board is used all over the world but various regions of Britain invented their own boards and some of these are still in use.

The East End or Fives board is the oddest of the regional boards and is found mainly in the East End of London. The numbering system is unique and it has a low number of segments which suggests that it may have been one of the earliest boards.

The Manchester or Log-end board is only 10in across and is supposed to be the most difficult board on which to play. This board is still popular, as its name implies, in Manchester and the surrounding area. There are no trebles and the numbers are arranged differently to the Standard board.

The Yorkshire board has no trebles or 25 segment but uses the standard numbering. It is used mainly in Yorkshire, Staffordshire and the North Midlands. An identical board is also used in Kent and called the Kent board.

The Tonbridge board is used in the Tonbridge-Sevenoaks area of Kent and is also called the Trebles board because what would be the doubles ring on a London board is used as the trebles ring. The numbering and dimensions are the same as the Standard board but there is no 25 segment and no outer trebles ring. The doubles on this board consist of triangles within the trebles ring and this calls for great accuracy.

The Staffordshire (or Burton) board is similar to the Yorkshire board but has a 25 segment and a unique feature—two beds outside the normal scoring area. These extra beds are in one-inch square diamonds between the 14 and 9 segments on the left and the 4 and 13 on the right. They are worth 25 each and can be used as a shot out. At one time this board was traditionally made from clay.

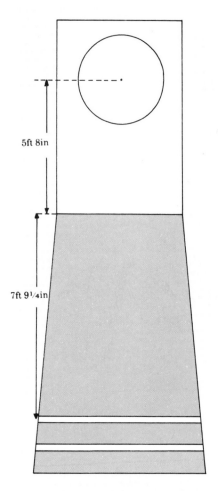

5ft 8in

7ft 9¼in

East End board

Manchester board

Yorkshire board

Tonbridge board

Staffordshire board

Club board

53

Technique

Technique is one of the most important aspects of darts, although every top professional would admit that Jocky Wilson's style makes a mockery of this. Wilson has the most unpretentious method imaginable—he walks to the oche, lines up his feet and throws. No attention to detail, no care, no fuss. Wilson's technique may be virtually non-existent, his style most ungainly. But there is no doubting its effectiveness; the clue, perhaps, to the whole question of technique, stance and grip. It is interesting that, with millions of players, no two people throw alike.

The Stance

The aim of most players is to keep their body still when they are throwing. John Lowe is considered the perfect example of this among the professionals. The only parts of the body which should move are the arm and wrist. The more the body moves in the fractions of a second before the dart is thrown, the greater the likelihood of inaccuracy.

Most players lean slightly forward in their natural stance at the oche—although some tend to stay more upright than others. Again, it is a matter of personal preference. The weight is balanced on one leg—for the right-handed thrower, the weight will naturally fall on the right foot and leg; for the left-hander, most weight is on the left leg.

Different speeds of delivery are unusual. But the ability to slow down or speed up according to the state of the match provides invaluable psychological ammunition. Some players become nervous as a match reaches its climax and want to get back to the board as soon as possible to try to finish off their opponent. If that opponent is cunning, he may try to delay his rival's return to the board for as long as possible, to prolong the tension.

Bristow is considered the master of this particular trick. He can throw extremely quickly or at a snail's pace, to suit his own requirements. But not many players attempt to alter their speed of play, still less consider it a part of their armour.

The Grip

It is said that no two players hold a dart in the same way. Considering that most darts are broadly similar in appearance, that may sound something of an exaggeration but it is so. Holding a dart comes naturally, rather like holding a pencil and there is no logical explanation for variations in the grip.

Three fingers are used: the thumb, index and third fingers. But spreading those fingers in different ways is part of the puzzle—pushing one further forward or back for personal comfort provides variety.

If the dart is held too far forward, there might be a loose grip on contact because of insufficient firmness in the thrust of the dart towards the board from the hand. A dart held too far forward is also more likely to tilt upwards in the board and, in that way, block the target area for the next dart. However, a dart held too far back down the barrel might dip too much in flight and enter the board at the opposite angle. Depending on the kind of stem and flights used, it is all a matter of finding the right balance.

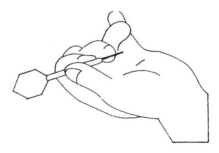

Linda Batten

Bobby George

People in the Media

The world of TV darts has given an opportunity to previously unknown characters to gain instant recognition as voices and names. The commentators who describe the action in televised competitions are a small band of enthusiasts who have become as famous as the players. People such as Tony Green and Sid Waddell can command respect and good fees throughout the world for their work.

Tony Green

When Eric Bristow and Maureen Flowers made a month's tour of Australia playing exhibition matches, Green went with them to enhance the professional coverage of the tour and add his own particular brand of commentary. Green even has his own agent—the same company which promotes darts players such as Bristow, Brown, Virachkul, Lord, Lazarenko and Maureen Flowers.

Calling out 'one hundred and eighty' in a Hull accent may seem a strange way to earn a handsome living. That was how Green's voice first became familiar to TV darts' fans.

Green, who is 42, played his darts for Lancashire for six years until 1980 but the boom in televised darts left him short of the time required for practice. He was also a master of ceremonies for many years and continues to combine that with commentating.

His compensation for forsaking that aspect of the game has been a worthwhile one, in terms of involvement and financial reward. A conservative estimate of his earnings for 1983 would be around the £60,000 mark—remarkable for a man who was once in the Hull Kingston Rovers Rugby League team and had trials for Yorkshire colts at cricket.

Green provides a good link between the game itself and the show-business razzamatazz which appears on TV. Indeed he is a paid-up member of the actors' union, Equity.

'Darts has been good to me,' he admits 'but remember, I have been throwing darts since I was fifteen. I know my way around a darts board and, since starting commentaries, I have made a special effort to learn all the positions from which players could go out. It's very useful to know what the players are likely to be aiming at. I have played against a lot of them, too, which has helped me learn each player's own favourite route to the winning double.'

Sid Waddell

Waddell is pure Geordie; that unmistakeable voice—full of life, character and excitement—has become a key ingredient in the world of darts. He has made a name for himself with pungent quips which provide accurate yet amusing summaries of the play.

Waddell's style is unique . . . TV shorthand he calls it. 'My comments have to be short and sharp but also sensible,' he says. This is never easy in the time allowed between players lining up their throws or changing places on the 'oche'.

Peter Purves

BBC's presentation work for darts is done by 44-year-old Peter Purves. His calmer tones provide the perfect contrast for the racy comments of Green and Waddell in the commentary box.

Purves did not have a darts background but approached the job in a solid, professional style, learning the game thoroughly and creating a personal friendship with many of the players, so that TV interviews were always informative and respected.

'I felt I had to earn the players' respect,' he said. The man who appeared for many years on the children's television programme *Blue Peter* has achieved that with some smooth performances.

Dave Lanning

Sid Waddell

People in the media/2

Purves' job might seem straightforward: a brief introduction before the action and, possibly, a short interview at the end of the game. But he takes a somewhat greater interest because he watches almost every game, looking for little pieces of information or action which he can mention in either his summary later or interview with the winner of the game.

Dave Lanning

Dave Lanning has established himself as the voice of Independent Television darts. Lanning has a rich accent—it was once described as a cross between Acker Bilk and Alf Garnett, because he hails from Poole in Dorset but has lived in Essex since 1960.

He also commentates on speedway and ice hockey for ITV—often in *World of Sport* on Saturdays. He has already seen vast technical improvements in the TV companies' coverage of darts. Independent Television were first to screen a tournament, the 1972 *News of the World* event. He believes that the game will continue to prosper, forcing television presentation to an even higher standard. 'Some people felt the darts bubble might burst but I do not see any likelihood whatsoever of that happening,' he says.

'Darts has changed a great deal from its early days of televised coverage. It used to be just a lot of fun but as with all ITV sport, it has become a lot more serious and professional. Darts supporters have also become more knowledgeable and technically minded since those early days. I also think that commentators have become more technically minded.

'I think we shall see more and more invention on the dartboard in the future. Games such as Around-the-Board are very possible, to add extra interest, rather than the sole sight of players throwing treble twenties

throughout each game.

'I believe the electronics world will help develop television coverage. The current method of commentators watching the board is fallible and the idea of an electronic board automatically lighting up a number is surely a logical extension, to help the viewer at home appreciate the game and see the action even earlier.'

Darts and TV have been closely linked to help each other in the game's rapid rise to popularity. That liaison seems sure to continue in the future to the benefit of both sides.

Tony Green

Nick Hunter, the BBC television producer who was one of the
first to see the potential of darts on the small screen.

Statistics

Counting shots

The ability to calculate quickly and accurately is most important for all players. Any player who finds difficulty with this basic skill starts with a disadvantage. This is another facet of the game which can be rapidly improved by regular practice. Learning to count up quickly and knowing your shots is half the battle.

A beginner should go systematically round the board to learn the position of all the numbers and the value of each number's double and treble; next the multiples of each number and what to aim for if you split a double. You will have noticed that the professional players aim mostly for the 20s segment of the board where they can earn the maximum score with three darts—180. However, as the numbers each side of the 20 segment are 1 and 5, a beginner would probably achieve higher scores initially be aiming for the lower left hand portion of the board where you can score between 11 and 19.

It is also important to practise finding your doubles as all games finish with a double shot and it is no good reducing your total quickly if you are unable to complete the game by scoring a double. Double 16 is a favourite finishing shot because if you miss it and score only 16, you still have the chance to go for double 8 and then double 4, etc.

Any score over 170 cannot be a game shot and a player should concentrate on bringing his total below that figure as quickly as possible. Below are some figures which it is worth memorising, for a standard game:

Highest score	180
Highest score with two darts	120
Highest score with one dart	60
Highest shot out	170

Highest shot out with two darts	110
Highest shot out with one dart	50
Lowest score not possible	163
Lowest two-dart score not possible	103
Lowest one-dart score not possible	23
Lowest shot out not possible	159
Lowest two-dart shot out not possible	99
Lowest even number not possible as game shot	162

Although there are an astonishing number of three-dart finishes—some 83,000—from a score of 170, the game-shot guide below gives the most popular finishes which can be learned by heart. You may find in time that you prefer a different finishing shot. All the professionals have their own favourite finishing routes and it is one task of the TV commentators to know those shots and where the players will aim from certain score.

100 and all numbers from 98 down to 41 can be scored in two darts; 50 and all even numbers below 41 can be scored with one dart; odd numbers below 40 (except 1) require two darts.

When calculating your finish—and should your opponent be handily placed to finish if you miss the out shot—always bring the bull into play. For example with 87 left—first dart 17^3 should single 17 be the score leaving 70, then second dart should be aimed at 20^3. Should you get single 20 then there is still an outshot on the bull.

Game shot guide

Key: 20^3 = treble twenty
20^2 = double twenty

With three darts:

170	$20^3, 20^3$, bull	131	$19^3, 14^3, 16^2$	69	$19^3, 6^2$
167	$20^3, 19^3$, bull	130	$20^3, 10^3, 20^2$	68	$20^3, 4^2$
164	$20^3, 18^3$, bull	129	$19^3, 16^3, 12^2$	67	$17^3, 8^2$
161	$20^3, 17^3$, bull	128	$18^3, 14^3, 16^2$	66	$15^2, 18^2$
160	$20^3, 20^3, 20^2$	127	$19^3, 10^3, 20^2$	66	$10^3, 18^2$
158	$18^3, 18^3$, bull	126	$19^3, 19$, bull	65	$25, 20^2$
158	$20^3, 20^3, 19^2$	125	$20^3, 25, 20^2$	64	$16^3, 8^2$
157	$19^3, 20^3, 20^2$	124	$20^3, 16^3, 8^2$	63	$17^3, 6^2$
156	$20^3, 20^3, 18^2$	123	$19^3, 10^3, 18^2$	62	$15^2, 16^2$
155	$20^3, 19^3, 19^2$	122	$18^3, 20^3, 4^2$	62	$10^3, 16^2$
154	$20^3, 18^3, 20^2$	121	$19^3, 16^3, 8^2$	61	$25, 18^2$
153	$20^3, 19^3, 18^2$	120	$20^3, 20, 20^2$	60	$20, 20^2$
152	$20^3, 20^3, 16^2$	119	$19^3, 10^3, 16^2$	59	$19, 20^2$
151	$20^3, 17^3, 20^2$	118	$20^3, 18, 20^2$	58	$18, 20^2$
150	$20^3, 18^3, 18^2$	117	$20^3, 17, 20^2$	57	$17, 20^2$
149	$20^3, 19^3, 16^2$	116	$20^3, 20, 18^2$	56	$16, 20^2$
148	$20^3, 16^3, 20^2$	115	$20^3, 15, 20^2$	55	$15, 20^2$
148	$20^3, 20^3, 14^2$	114	$20^3, 18, 18^2$	54	$18, 18^2$ or $14, 20^2$
147	$20^3, 17^3, 18^2$	113	$20^3, 13, 20^2$	53	$13, 20^2$
146	$20^3, 18^3, 16^2$	112	$20^3, 20, 16^2$	52	$20, 16^2$ or $12, 20^2$
145	$20^3, 15^3, 20^2$	111	$19^3, 18, 18^2$	51	$19, 16^2$ or $11, 20^2$
144	$20^3, 16^3, 18^2$	110	$20^3, 18, 16^2$	50	$18, 16^2$ or $10, 20^2$
144	$20^3, 20^3, 12^2$	109	$19^3, 20, 16^2$	49	$17, 16^2$ or $9, 20^2$
143	$20^3, 17^3, 16^2$	108	$20^3, 16, 16^2$	48	$16, 16^2$ or $8, 20^2$
142	$20^3, 14^3, 20^2$	107	$19^3, 18, 16^2$	47	$15, 16^2$ or $7, 20^2$
141	$20^3, 19^3, 12^2$	106	$20^3, 10, 18^2$	46	$14, 16^2$ or $6, 20^2$
140	$20^3, 16^3, 16^2$	105	$19^3, 8, 20^2$	45	$13, 16^2$ or $5, 20^2$
139	$20^3, 13^3, 20^2$	104	$18^3, 18, 16^2$	44	$12, 16^2$ or $4, 20^2$
138	$20^3, 14^3, 18^2$	103	$19^3, 6, 20^2$	43	$11, 16^2$ or $3, 20^2$
137	$20^3, 15^3, 16^2$	102	$20^3, 10, 16^2$	42	$10, 16^2$ or $2, 20^2$
136	$20^3, 20^3, 8^2$	101	$19^3, 12, 16^2$	41	$9, 16^2$ or $1, 20^2$
135	$19^3, 14^3, 18^2$	99	$19^3, 10, 16^2$		
134	$20^3, 14^3, 16^2$				
133	$19^3, 18^2, 20^2$				
132	$20^3, 20^2, 16^2$				

With two darts:

110	20^3, bull	92	$20^3, 16^2$	80	$16^3, 16^2$
107	19^3, bull	91	$17^3, 20^2$	79	$17^3, 14^2$
104	18^3, bull	90	$18^3, 18^2$	78	$18^3, 12^2$
101	17^3, bull	89	$19^3, 16^2$	77	$19^3, 10^2$
100	$20^3, 20^2$	88	$16^3, 20^2$	76	$20^3, 18^2$
98	$20^3, 19^2$	87	$17^3, 18^2$	75	$15^3, 15^2$
97	$19^3, 20^2$	86	$18^3, 16^2$	74	$14^3, 16^2$
96	$20^3, 18^2$	85	$15^3, 20^2$	73	$19^3, 8^2$
95	$19^3, 19^2$	84	$20^3, 12^2$	72	$16^3, 12^2$
94	$18^3, 20^2$	83	$17^3, 16^2$	71	$13^3, 16^2$
93	$19^3, 18^2$	82	$14^3, 20^2$	70	$15^3, 20^2$
		81	$15^3, 18^2$		

Results

World championships

1978	L Rees
1979	J Lowe
1980	E Bristow
1981	E Bristow
1982	J Wilson
1983	K Deller

World masters

1978	J Lowe
1979	C Lazarenko
1980	J Lowe
1981	E Bristow
1982	D Whitcombe

Nations cup

1978	Sweden
	(S Lord, K Ohlsson, B Enquvist)
1979	England
	(E Bristow, T Brown, J Lowe)
1980	England
	(E Bristow, T Brown, J Lowe)
1981	Scotland
	(A Ross, R Smith, J Wilson)
1982	England
	(E Bristow, B George, J Lowe)
1983	England
	(E Bristow, J Lowe, D Whitcombe)

World Cup

1977	Wales
	(A Evans, D Jones, L Rees)
	Singles: L Rees
1979	England
	(J Lowe, E Bristow, T Brown, B Lennard)
	Singles: L Virachkul
1981	England
	(E Bristow, T Brown, C Lazarenko, J Lowe)
	Singles: J Lowe

Europe cup

1978	England
1980	England
1982	England (men)
	Wales (women)

Men's international rankings (May 1983)

1	E Bristow,	49 pts
2	J Wilson,	38
3	J Lowe,	31½
4	C Lazarenko,	28½
5	D Whitcombe,	27½
6	B George	26
7	T Brown,	21
8	K Deller,	19
9	S Lord,	18½
10	N Virachkul,	18

British open (men)

1978	E Bristow
1979	T Brown
1980	C Lazarenko
1981	E Bristow
1982	J Wilson
1983	E Bristow

British open (women)

1979	J Campbell
1980	L Batten
1981	A M Davies
1982	M Flowers
1983	S Earnshaw

British matchplay

1978	J Lowe
1979	C Lazarenko
1980	J Wilson
1981	J Wilson
1982	E Bristow

British international championship

	Men	Women
1979	England	England
1980	England	England
1981	Wales	Scotland
1982	England	England
1983	England	England

Winmau World masters

Embassy World championship

Acknowledgements

We would like to thank Olly Croft and his staff at the British Darts Organisation, Tony Green and Dave Lanning, who have all been invaluable in supplying advice and information, and generous in giving their time. We are also grateful to the BDO and the BBC Hulton Picture Library in supplying additional photographs.

Olly Croft, one of the key figures in the modern darts boom. He was a founder member of the British Darts Organisation in 1973 and he has kept his finger on the pulse as general secretary of the BDO and the World Darts Federation.

Louise Brannon
was
the
25/11/85
Friday,